GREEN CARD:

THE UNTOLD STORIES

Dr. Donette Wright

ISBN: 9798784072252 (paperback)

Printed in the United States of America.

Dedication

I want to dedicate this book to ***Bishop Reverend Dr. Sylvester Wright.***

Dr. Bishop Sylvester Wright is a mentor, friend, spiritual father, and a good person to me. God bless this man of God in my life.

I remember when I needed a pastor and much encouragement. My faith was being tested; it wasn't peaches and cream. One morning I was going to church, and my car would not start, so I sat in the car and went live on social media. I was sharing what I was going through, and he was watching me conducting a service all by myself, and he had a good laugh. He laughed so hard that he made me laugh. I understand now that he was giving me a revelation to smile at the storm.

It wasn't always laughing for him; sometimes, it was strictly business. Dr. Wright has a ministry overseas in Pakistan, Kenya, Maryland, Pennsylvania, etc.

Sir, I am glad you are in my life. Thank you for pushing me to the next level.

Acknowledgments

There are some special people I want to take time out to thank for making this project a reality.

Thanks to my children, Krystal Wright, Savione Wright, and Joshua Ricketts Junior.

To my spiritual son and daughter, Andrew Powell and Prophetess Deborah Henry, thank you.

Thanks to my siblings, Hillary Wright-Williams, Allison Wright-Morris, Alton Eddie Wright, and Tomnisha Wright-Harry.

Thanks to my prayer partners: my spiritual mother, Daphne Barnett, Pastor Karen

Levine, Minister Ingrid Facey and Yvonne Fawcett.

Thanks to my best friends, Dr. Archbishop Chief Apostle Raleigh Christie and Bonita Daily-Anderson.

These people are very significant in my life and I want to thank them for the roles they have played in my success.

Table of Contents

Preface

I want to start a candid discussion on the real stories out there of those who endured hell to get a green card. The question one must ask themselves is, "Is it worth it?" I would agree that there is no glory without sacrifice, but the level of compromise and sacrifice our brothers and sisters, particularly our women, have had to endure will cause one to wonder.

There are legal ways to get a green card and, like everything else, there are other ways. There are many arranged marriages where citizens will take money and get married so one can get their green card. This is actually a felony. A citizen who is being used for papers can also be charged with a federal crime.

Life is built on choices, and sometimes we need the relevant information before we make certain decisions. This is called making a calculated decision.

These conversations are somewhat censored, but the stories are real, and the characters are real people. The situations described actually happened, which means someone had to endure some terrible storms with the hope of a better day. For some, the better day came, but others got stuck in a perpetual nightmare.

Names and situations were changed or modified to protect the integrity and character of those involved.

Let's talk.

Introduction

Having the knowledge of what people are willing to do to get a green card can have you standing at an altar, questioning if the marriage you are about to enter into is a marriage of convenience. The reality is, if the marriage is for that secret purpose, then the marriage will not last. One may walk away with legal standings in a country not of his/her birth, but someone, maybe an entire family, will be left broken and possibly traumatized. This is my story, but it is also the story of many people I know and some I don't know.

I have stood at an altar myself, and experienced the same doubtful thoughts going through my head. I still went ahead, with only a glimmer of hope that it would work out for my good. It didn't. It took me up to five years to make the decision to sponsor him, my own husband. If I knew then what I know now, I would have walked away instantly. It was a very good marriage; he was a good husband and a provider, but it doesn't excuse the fact that a green card was the goal.

As a citizen of a country, you can sponsor an immigrant to stay in the country or even to migrate to the country. There may not be any other way for such a person to get to, for example, the United States of America. The green card is given to potential citizens because of some connection to someone already there, unless it is a long-term in-demand work program, for example, nursing and teaching. Citizens have the power to create green card holders, and people seeking an opportunity to leave their country behind for greener pastures are very much aware of this. So, if someone is showing interest, the true motive is not immediately apparent.

I have seen many different sides to this reality. Even people you think love you or claim to love you may just be pretending for what they can get.

I have been there, and the stories I share are of real people who have also had a similar experience.

I pray that this narrative will open our eyes to a much deeper truth: if we have to do something illegal or damage families to migrate from our country to another country, then there may be a possibility that we were not meant to migrate. When the time is right, an opportunity will present itself that will ensure you maintain the integrity of your soul. If someone should ask me if it was worth it, my answer would be no.

I worked in the hair salon industry for over fifteen-plus years and listened to different stories of women and men who have to go through a tremendous amount of struggles to get a green card.

One of my aunts was the first person I saw who did a green card for someone. It was never in her favour.

My mother married her partner for love, and it turned out that it was only for a green card for himself and his children.

One of my dearest friends, whose name I will withhold, went through the same trauma to obtain her green card.

In this book, I will be sharing personal experiences all in the name of a green card. Some of the names I will withhold, though I have permission from the parties to share the in-depth story of rape, abuse, sodomy, working like a slave, being called many things, working different jobs but having no access to their monies...and this list is not exhaustive.

I have seen a friend promised love, but it was a marriage for papers. Some marriages still did not provide the experience of the American dream because they still did not get a green card. Many have been blackmailed by threats to call I.C.E. to have them removed from the house and country, even though they both purchased with both names on everything.

There are those who have mothered a child in the name of a green card and were still given the raw end of the stick because they still did not obtain a green card, yet they have to play the role of a mother to children. She had no idea her sponsor had other baby mothers and children hanging on to the same promise.

One friend met her husband, who said the first time he laid eyes on her, he knew she was going to be his wife; however, he spoke very little English. She encouraged herself to understand the love of her life, and wanting to have fluent dialogue with him, she learned the language. After finding out that her husband had a whole entire family in another country, she had nowhere else to go, so she was forced to do things outside her morals, all in the name of becoming a legal resident in America.

I remember traveling to the United States and overstaying my visa, thinking that JAMAICA was too difficult and too hard to live. I thought it was going to be easy to become a legal resident of the United States of America. I was mistaken. The price I had to pay was astronomical and extremely painful, and never-ending. I am still living the nightmare, even as I pen these words.

I remember someone coming to this country as a child because her mother passed away. Her father, during the green card process, left her on her own with family members who were unable to sponsor her. She was at the age where she could date, so she got a boyfriend, thinking that would be a win. She experienced motherhood at the age of fourteen, and that came with years of abuse: mental, physical, and emotional. She later got married to him and had two children. Eventually, she obtained her green card. They are still married to this day, though maybe not happily. She was a mother at the age of fourteen. Was it really worth it?

Chapter One

Ally's Story

Ally got married to a gentleman from another country who claimed to have spoken no English; however, he took English classes and started speaking English. Whenever he communicated on the phone, he spoke in his native dialect. By this time, they moved in together and were living together as man and wife.

Miss Ally found out later that this man had a full family back in his country and had no intention of being with her. She considered him her husband and lifelong partner; however, Miss Ally was undocumented in the United States of America, so he promised her that he would make sure to give her legal documents.

Miss Ally worked two jobs; she pulled more weight to make sure the house was provided for. He drove a nice car; he had money in his pocket as his good wife provided. Whenever he was having a conversation on the phone, Ally would do everything to listen. She understood nothing he said because he would never speak English around her.

I was Miss Ally's hairdresser, so on many occasions, she and I would have a long conversation, and she would confide some of the stuff that was going on to me, which I will not divulge in the book. I want to keep it on a green card issue situation.

Miss Ally went on with life as usual, even though she was dying inside and not understanding a word he said because he was speaking in his native dialect. Miss Ally decided to start recording with a hidden voice-activated recorder. Miss Ally wondered how and who would translate the entire conversation. She was recording on a daily basis consistently for years. Miss Ally would later find out that this man had no plans of helping her as he described her as his "human donkey" that was working to take care of his family back home. He had no intention of giving her full status.

Miss Ally took matters into her own hands after finding out what he was constantly talking about on the phone. She moved her mailing address to a PO Box and continued in the relationship as if she knew nothing. Later on, her documents would come in the mail, and she would sign his name where it was needed. All her documents were being processed, so the cat and mouse game had been going on underneath his nose. He had no idea.

Eventually, the donkey quit doing everything and carrying all the weight and he did not know. When the legs from the donkey fell out, Ally collected her green card, social security card, and all her documents, and she moved out of the apartment and left him there.

Miss Ally had received her green card and no longer needed to be in that situation.

I would not consider that as being her using him; I would say that was an even ride.

Chapter Two

Ms. Kelly's Story

Ms. Kelly met and got married Mr. Kent in 1987. She migrated to the United States in 1986. She sponsored her husband and his children. In the United States, they lived together for approximately eight or nine years, at which point he had an affair, and the marriage went down the tubes, and he left.

They rekindled their relationship and came back together, and he left again. Soon after, his children moved out of the house because they were the ones who had brought them together, and he never came back. That was it. All he wanted from Ms. Kelly was a green card because after he got the green card, he was a totally different person. She had to put up with a lot of disrespect, more infidelity, disrespect from the children, and so on.

They had properties together, both in Jamaica and the United States, which made it very difficult for the divorce to happen. Ms. Kelly did not believe in divorce, so she stayed in the dormant marriage; she stayed in the marriage for at least twenty-five more years at which point she became sick. She still pushed through, despite how sick she was.

Ms. Kelly made a house in Jamaica; she owned a house in Dallas. These were properties they accumulated together in the marriage. Before she passed away, she made a will, and she willed one of the properties to him. Even on her deathbed, he wanted her to sign things over to him.

I felt like the green card should have been enough for him and his children, and he was undeserving of anything more. He should have taken his green card and gone about his business, but he went to the hospital while Ms. Kelly was battling leukaemia and wanted her to sign over the rest of her properties to him. At this point, she did not do that. So, he did not come to her funeral.

She passed away, and that was the end of him. They were still married, so her property was legally his. So, the fight for the property continued in court; he still did not go away. He is still fighting, period.

Chapter Three

Nardia's Story

Nardia is an amazing woman; one of my favourite people. She worked at the Sangster's Bookstore for years. This is one person who introduced me to reading. This is the person who, whenever our book lists would come, she would be the person mom would give the book lists to, and I would get all my books. She played a very important part in my life. Hence, the reason when she was used for a green card, it affected me the way it did.

She migrated from Jamaica to live in the United States. However, she went to Jamaica and met a police officer. We are going to call him Mike Harris. They got married; he had four children. She sponsored him and his four children.

When we came here, it was me, my mom and his four children. As a matter of fact, my mom brought his children up when we were coming up together. Later on, after they got here, that marriage dissolved in five years. He got his green card and, again, I believe that that was what he really wanted.

Before the green card, it was bliss. It was marital bliss, they were so in love; everything was amazing. It was awesome. He got a two-year temporary green card, and it was wonderful. He went in for the second half, got the green card, and he became a new person. He was one of the most disrespectful people on earth; there was also infidelity. I know Nardia is yet to share some of the things she went through. It is not easy to talk about the nightmares we sometimes experience because of a choice we made.

Most people do not share what they go through in the green card process; they stay in it for different reasons. Some are trapped. Some are threatened. They will go through it because most of the time they do not want their family to know. I knew how unhappy she was. She had been through a lot of failed relationships, and this time, this was a marriage she wanted to hold on to. So a lot of things went on that I am pretty sure she is yet to talk about.

I saw her face; I observed countenance; I knew her, I knew the person who used to work at Sangster's Bookstore. I knew who used to bring me bubbles and clips. I knew who used to bring me books to read. I knew who used to bring me books that I used water to paint, and the paint would come through. I knew who this woman was. So, when she changed, I knew that she was very,

very hurt by this marriage. Again, it was a green card deal, and he was gone.

Of course, the person he cheated on her with, he ended up marrying her, and it did not work out.

Nardia did get married again, and this time it was different.

Chapter Four

November's Story

November was severely obese, and at her heaviest; she was close to 500 pounds. She was in and out of the hospital where they were trying to control her diet with a different meal plan, so she had to spend a lot of time in the hospital. She lived in the South Bronx. She was an only child; however, she migrated from Jamaica when she was fourteen years old.

Because of her size, I believe she was very insecure. So, when love came her way, she would take it from anyone, whichever way she needed to take it. This awesome and amazing, six foot two, very, very good-looking suave came her way. She was told that she could never have any children; however, she got pregnant by him at her heaviest, and they had a son. She had that baby prematurely, and the gentleman could not handle it. I am going to call him Evan.

Evan could not handle it, so he just dipped. That damaged her severely, and she had to handle that on her own.

One of her sons died. I still remember going to his funeral to this day. So, in her mourning and grieving, she met another suave who swooped into her life and just scooped her up and comforted her. He was in the country illegally, I mean undocumented. I do not like to say illegal; he was undocumented and treated her wonderful, and they got married.

Out of that marriage came two children. November did weight loss surgery, and she lost all that weight. I think she lost that weight and found herself. Anyway, she started gaining confidence in who she is. She ended up marrying this guy, and she gave him a green card. After he got his green card, he became a different person; very verbally abusive. I do not know if there was physical abuse; she never said, but I know he was verbally abusive.

He cheated with multiple different persons. There were times where she would have me call him to see if he would take the bait, and he took it; hook, line and sinker. He would set up dates that he would meet with me. I asked him if he had a wife, and he said no.

"Why don't you have a wife?" I would ask. He would avoid the question.

It was only for a green card. He got the green card, and he just shot it, yet they had two children together: a son and a daughter. All he wanted to deal with was his son and his daughter, and that was it.

She did not remarry. She is now living her life. Now, this is one person who I know that a green card "situationship" damaged her for good. She hit the bottle; she drinks very hard. She has never been the same after that.

Chapter Five

Claire's Story

Claire is on her third marriage for her green card, and she has been in the United States for years, more than twenty years. She worked as a CNA, did live-in jobs, and saved a lot of money. She was used quite a bit because she was very quiet. She is one of those passive kinds of people.

People would often borrow money from her because she always had cash. She is undocumented, so she does not do bank accounts and all those things. She saved money with a "su-su" partner like it is called. So, she loaned money a lot to people, and she never got it back. She is a super nice woman, so she was set up, introduced to this guy for him to marry her.

Initially, it was supposed to be a business wedding. After he saw her picture, he said no business wedding, he wanted her to be his wife. He wanted a real marriage. So she said fine; they were going to have a real marriage. After they dated for a few months or so, he decided that he was going to marry her. He took her to the bank, and they opened an account. He put his name on the account because of her status. This was for her to have direct deposit from her job to go into this account. She had no more access to her account again. He had access to all her money.

This man worked for the airport, the airline industry. He could fly every weekend if he wanted to, and he would make use of it. Whenever he went on those trips, and whenever she checked the account, hotels would be on there.

This man would just have fun with this woman's money, and she could not say anything because he already married her. She was his wife.

He decided that they were going to buy a home together. They went house hunting. He would see homes, pick out different homes, send her the pictures of the homes and tell her to choose the one she wanted.

Whenever she chose one, he said he did not like it. Then finally, he decided that he did not want to live in New York anymore. So, he moved away from New York and just abandoned her. She would not settle for just being abandoned while this man had access to all her money. He moved to a different state, and she followed him.

She packed her stuff in a truck and paid thousands to follow him. He bought a house; the day of the closing, he told her she did not have to come, but not in so many words. He was very explicit, like, "You're an idiot. Where are you going? You don't have social security number; you don't have any green card. Where are you going to go sign for the house?"

She had $30,000 in the bank account, and it was all going into this house buying situation where her name was not going to be on anything. This man then forced himself on her and raped her. Whenever he wanted to have sex with her, and she would say no—this woman was barely 110-pounds in weight—this man was about 300 pounds, about six feet, five inches—he would just rip her clothes off. All different kinds of sex: anal sex, oral sex, any hole she had, he was in there.

This went on for years. It would go on to the point where she would just lay there, and he did not care. She would say to him, "I'm tired of being raped for a green card." Anyhow, she still stuck it out that he would stop, and he still did not stop. So, they moved.

I hate to talk about it. They moved, and it got worse. She could not have anyone come over; could not keep the lights on. He walked around and turned off the lights. He told her that he had lost one home before, and he was not losing this one so she could get out. He threw her out multiple different times because she had no proof that her money went into this house.

She went to close out the account; they told her that she could not close the account because she did not hold the account. He just used up all her money. The lady who she was taking care of died, so now she did not have a job. She could not turn the lights on in the house. Everything she did was a problem for him. She could not close the door. Sometimes she was watching TV, and he disconnected the cable wires and packed up all the cable boxes.

Then whenever he wanted sex, he would plug back everything in, rape again, sodomize again; it was just horrible. No friends could go there; her friends could not go there. I remember going there, and he cussed me out and put me out. Twice, he put me out, so I decided I was not going back to his house again. He just had her boxed in by herself.

The last thing he told her was that he was never giving her a green card. But then he told her the $30,000 that he used to buy the house was his pay for the green card. He would give her the green card, and she should just leave. She said no because green card for sale is illegal; it is a federal crime. Not only could she be charged, but he could be charged. So they were going back and forth; she did not get the green card, and she was not getting out of the house.

She was not leaving because that was her money, and it was his green card.

I do not know how that story will end, but I know the price for that green card was a lot, a whole lot, period.

Chapter Six

Oprah's Story

Oprah and I have been friends for over twenty-three years. She met this man just as he came from Jamaica. Unbeknownst to her, he was undocumented as well. He was very nice, treated her well. He was an awesome husband in the beginning. Because he had no documents, he was one of those guys who stayed home and cooked and did the laundry and did all those wonderful things.

She believed that she met her prince; her knight in shining armour, and they have a son together. She went to the point where she put his name on her neck, and that was how much they were in love. They got married, and the marriage lasted maybe a good ten years until he got his green card. And after he got his green card, she helped him to sponsor his two sons. So, after his two sons got their green cards and they came from Jamaica, that was when it started.

She found pictures on his phone. He had slept with all her girlfriends. He no longer cared about taking care of the home or doing the stuff that he used to do anymore. He was just a different person; he was highly disrespectful. They started fighting, like physical fistfights, and this just went on and on. There are times when they would call me, and I would go in and do counseling. I would sit them individually because I really wanted their marriage to work.

I did not want it to be just a green card thing because he and I had become very good friends. He had one foot out and one foot in because after a while he did not want to hear me anymore, but I still tried. Eventually, they had this big blow up, and he called her a roach. I will never forget it. She said to him, "A roach can't give somebody a green card." She told him he had to go, so she packed him up and put him out. He went and started staying with different women, different girls all over the place.

He would come by the house with the different girls, and she would tell him that she didn't want them around her son. You know how women can get when different women come around their children, and that brought about another drama with him being with different females; it was just ridiculous. They were separated for more than six years.

This man started working at this awesome job where he had a life insurance policy, medical benefits, and she was the beneficiary because they were still legally married; there was no divorce. One day he went in and changed it; took her off the insurance, took her off as beneficiary. She found out she was no longer a beneficiary at his funeral.

One night he was coming home from work, and he was super tired. He checked into this hotel to get some sleep. While he checked into the hotel, he did not even put his bags or anything down. There was a knock on the door, and he thought it was someone from the front desk. He opened the door, and there were four persons standing on the other side. They opened fire; six shots, three in his head and some more in his chest and he died in the hotel. She got the phone call that he was murdered. His killers were captured on video. They eventually caught them but they are not charged yet; they are still in jail awaiting trial to at writing of this book.

So the long and short of this one is, a green card really did nothing for him because his next trip back to Jamaica with the green card from the roach was in a casket. That same roach took him back to Jamaica and buried him. When she flew down, she got married and came back with a new husband.

Chapter Seven

Dad's Story

My mom and dad were married when they were eighteen. Out of that marriage came four children. He had an older daughter, Hilary Wright. My mom and dad divorced, but I do not remember the year. My mom remarried, and dad remained single.

My dad was here for quite some years, but he was undocumented. My grandmother sponsored us and sponsored my mom. Because my mom and dad were still married, my mom added him to our filing. My dad had to fly back to Jamaica. On his way back to Jamaica, all he had to do was tell the immigration that he was in America illegally and he was going home. They were not going to stop him.

He went to Jamaica, picked up his papers, and returned to the United States with us because my mom sponsored him. After they got back here, they divorced.

My dad remained single for a while. He was never dating anyone. Eventually, dad went back to Jamaica and found this lady; they were together. They dated at some point. He contacted this woman in Jamaica, who contacted someone else, and the next thing I knew, my dad was getting married. I flew down for the wedding; it was a beautiful wedding. He sponsored her. When she got here, she was a nice wife; she cooked dinner, and so on.

She found out the quarter was different from the nickel and the dime, meaning, she knew how to take the train now and the bus. She knew her way to Brooklyn because that was what really happened. Once they knew the difference between the quarter, the dime, and the nickel, and then knew their way by train around Brooklyn, they were fully Americanized. They were good. She worked ten jobs. She worked in the school system. She worked every day. She worked on the weekends, and she worked twice during the week, but dad did not see a dime.

All her money was sent to Jamaica. She started building a house; my dad did not know. She had taxis on the road; my dad did not know. She sponsored her children; my dad did not know. She was just doing things, and my dad had no idea. He would just hear things second-hand, and then he would go and check it out to see if it was real. So yes, it was real. She was treating him so badly. I could not allow my father to go through that anymore.

I applied for a retirement home in Delaware where I lived, and he was qualified for the retired home. I moved him to the retirement home and left her in New York, and that was the end of that situation.

I knew that she only wanted a green card, and she was a younger woman. My dad was an older guy for her. So, she was not doing anything for him as it was. So why have her there, not doing anything for him while he was paying all the rent? The rent was $1200, and it took all his little pension money, while all her money was going to Jamaica to put taxis on the road, build a big house, and taking care of her children. That was not fair.

So, if I had to step in and do something about that green card "situationship," I was going to do something about it. My dad was extremely happy living in a nice retirement home; he can stay there until his eyes close. That was the end of their story. She did not reach out to him and does not act as if she wanted him back. She does not try to see him. She does not want to know where the address is. She will not tell him where she lives. So that is that; it was nothing but a green card situation.

Chapter Eight

Ms. Sharp's Story

Ms. Sharp went to Jamaica to minister at a revival. The revival was for two weeks. There was a guy who was playing for her on the third night. She turned to one of her girlfriends and said, "The person who is playing the keyboard, his head is shaped like an egg." They laughed about it. In the meantime, he was telling his friends that he wanted to meet the lady who was preaching.

Anyway, her spiritual father at the time introduced them. He was shaking her hand, and he would not let it go. So Ms. Sharp said,

"Can I have my hand back?" He let her hand go. The next night the musician came back, and he played for her again. Then he said, "I am going to marry you."

Ms. Sharp replied, "You're kidding. You have to be kidding me."

She was a few years older than this person, so it just did not make any sense. It was not going to happen; she was not doing it.

Ms. Sharp had decided that she did not want any more children, and she knew this person had no kids. He asked to take her out on a date. Her Bishop at the time arranged for them to go out. They rented a car and all that, so they had a ride, and he took her out.

They were walking on the beach, and she had some ankle wrap sandals on, heels on, and he took them off. He wrapped them up and threw them over his shoulder as they were walking on the beach.

He asked her, "What do you want me to do for you for the rest of your life?"

She said, "I want flowers every Saturday."

He said he would stay in Jamaica and send her flowers every Saturday. The date went on. They went out again and kept going out on dates.

Before she left Jamaica, they had an argument. They had a heated argument, and she was just so upset, so she walked away from him and left shortly afterward.

When she came home, she was at her girlfriend's house, and he called and said, "I can't afford to lose you."

Ms. Sharp was like, "This doesn't make any sense. I don't want to do this."

He proposed, "Would you marry me?"

Ms. Sharp flew back to Jamaica three months later, and they got engaged. In another six months, they were married. She did not sponsor him until about five years later. She just would not do it. She did everything to not do it.

When this guy was going to the United States Embassy in Jamaica, there was a flood, and their car almost got washed away. Everything that could have happened for him not to come to the States happened. Anyway, he finally got through. When he went to the embassy, he got a full visa. He did not get one where you get two years, and you have to go back in again. He got a full green card, and he came to the States.

After he got here, they had an amazing marriage. Ms. Sharp had an awesome marriage. He was an amazing husband. They had a baby. However, the sex was not every night; that was not there, so he started venting at work to someone else about what was going on in the marriage. Whoever he was venting to decided to fill Ms. Sharp's spot, and they ended up sleeping together. Ms. Sharp found out about it.

Ms. Sharp called the girl, and the girl was telling her, "Yes, I slept with him in your car" and the whole enchilada, and it got really muddy. Ms. Sharp did not want to do the whole back and forth with her, so she just told her, "He's your husband now." The car she said she slept with him in, Ms. Sharp called her best friend and asked, "Do you want a car?" She gave the car to the girl because she was never going to drive the car again. He used to drive that car because Ms. Sharp had two cars when he came here. So, she said to her best friend, "Take a car, take the car."

Ms. Sharp could not do it. They decided to go to counseling, and he started denying that it had happened. They went to counseling in Brooklyn. Pastor Rattray was their counselor, and they went to Brooklyn repeatedly. He kept denying what he did, so Ms. Sharp hired a private investigator. The private investigator got all the information that was needed to prove that he was cheating. The private investigator got proof of everything her husband was doing. That was when he admitted that he did it while in a counseling session. Ms. Sharp was done; right there and then, she knew that she was done.

They kept living in the same house, and they kept arguing back and forth. One day, there was this big blow up. She said to him, "Go on about your business and leave me alone." He took it that she threw him out of her house.

You know when birds want to go south, they wait for wind, and that was what she thought he was waiting for. He packed his stuff and left. After he left, that was it. He came back home again, and he was trying. By the time he came home and wanted to try, she already made up her mind that she was going to move away.

Eventually, she wanted to try the marriage again. She wanted to believe that this was not a green card thing. She wanted to believe that. They had a son together. When she met this guy, he did not have a high school diploma. He had nothing. He became an LPN, then he became an RN. Then he became a nurse preceptor, where he taught the new nurses who came in. He worked in the emergency room somewhere in New York— she will not say the hospital.

Ms. Sharp wanted to believe that her marriage was real and that it was not a green card thing. But she knew in her heart of hearts; she felt like it was a green card opportunity because had it not been for her, this man would have never been in this country because he had no family here. So that was about it. There was no trying on his part. Ms. Sharp said, "You cannot work the same job with this woman who you cheat with and claim we are working on this marriage. You have to leave the job. You cannot work a job with her."

He said, "I just bought a new car, and I cannot afford to get rid of this car."

So because he just bought a new car, he could not leave the job. Ms. Sharp said, "Okay, keep the job; I'm leaving." She left, and moved to Delaware, bought a house, and never went back, and that was the end of it.

Ms. Sharp did not remarry. He remarried, and it lasted for three years and ended in a divorce. He is now going on to his third marriage.

Chapter Nine

Is It Really Worth It?

Through my own personal experience, and the experiences of all those whose stories I have shared, and the countless others whose stories may never be told, I learned some very valuable lessons. There is a saying that experience teaches wisdom. The challenge I find when dealing with people is, are you willing to learn from other people's experiences, or are you adamant to learn your own lessons via your own experiences? There is wisdom from other people's stories that can aid us in not wasting many years and not getting perpetually locked into a nightmare.

People repeat too many mistakes, when the knowledge and wisdom exist for them to avoid certain pitfalls.

If somebody comes to Jamaica and you ask them something, and if they say that they do not have it, do not have this disgusting comeback. Sometimes they really truly do not have it. Not everyone who migrates is living the American dream. There are many who are living a nightmare. If you ask somebody for a t-shirt, if they give you a Fruit of the Loom and not a Gucci t-shirt, be grateful for the Fruit of the Loom that they gave you because they themselves do not have a Gucci t-shirt.

If they have the Gucci t-shirt and give you the Fruit that Looms, you do not know what they went through to buy themselves the Gucci t-shirt. So whatever they give you, be grateful for it because the things that some people have to go through to stay in this country, it is not normal, and it is surely not easy. The average person would quit; the average person would go back to Jamaica; the average person would surrender. This path is not for everybody, and it was not designed for anyone. We created that path, and those who choose to walk it must pay the price.

Many people had to leave their green card marriage; the marriage where the green card was promised. Sometimes people pay people to do it, but that is illegal. Sometimes people pay to get their green card, but the person they pay to get the green card still wants to have all kinds of kinky sex with them, and if they do not agree to do these things, they walk away.

Some people may wonder, "How have you been in America for so long and still haven't gotten your green card?" Well, you do not know why they did not get the green card yet. You do not know why they did not get their citizenship yet. You do not know why they are still undocumented. The answer is, because they are not willing to compromise. They are not willing to put their bodies through the things the sponsor was going to put them through.

So be grateful for whatever anybody in America gives to you. If they say they do not have it, trust them that they do not have it; believe them that they do not have it. We not only struggle from "Oh, it's cold in America," but there are a myriad of other struggles to endure. Some of these struggles are untold. Some struggles are disgusting. Some of the struggles are painful. Some struggles lasts for years; some of these struggles lead to mental illness; some to death.

A lot of women are suffering from mental illness from green card trauma that they never really get over. Some people never learn to trust again after green card trauma. Some people are here, and they are married two, three, and four times for a green card.

I have a girlfriend who married four times for a green card, and she still did not get it. Family members have died since she has been here. Her mother, father, sister, and brother died; the car ran off Flat Bridge; her family members died, and she could not attend the funeral. I can only imagine how much time she went through the process to get her green card.

So green card drama has a lot of untold stories, and I hope this book will help people to come forward and share their experiences so it can help others. People in Jamaica or in any other country are naïve. I can talk about Jamaica because they are my people. But this is a reality for many people in different countries; talk about it. I want it to be an open dialogue because people do not understand that when you say you do not have it, you actually do not have it. I really do not have it. Hear me when I say, "I don't have it."

So do not tell me you have been here for how many years, but you still take the train. You do not know my story. Hear me when I say, "I don't own a home." You do not know my story. There is a reason why I do not have a husband; you do not know my story.

"So why are you not married yet?"

You do not know my story.

"Why don't you have a big bank account?"

You do not know my story.

"Why didn't you come back to Jamaica and visit again?"

You do not know my story.

I share people's stories so you can get the opportunity to rewrite your own story or just change the narrative. There is a strong message in the stories themselves. You do not know what people have been through to be where they are. So sometimes we who are standing on the outside should lower our expectations because the perception is that others are living in the land of opportunity so they must have it, for they have somehow arrived.

The reality is, a lot of people put themselves through a lot of stuff just to be able to be there documented; it is not necessarily that they have made it. I am a voice for those people issuing a warning. Even now, I know that there are people who have that desire to go into arranged marriages and do whatever it takes to get a green card, but I do not think there is anything much out there that would kind of signal a warning to say: maybe you should not go down that road because you do not know what you are about to take on.

Let this book serve as a warning to you.

To those who are in these kinds of marriages, I will share a word with you in another chapter.

To those who have managed to walk away from these marriages and are standing on the outside, alone and traumatized, I will share a word with you too.

The struggle is real, but we can overcome. It is much easier not to have made this decision than it is to deal with the repercussions of it. Know that there is healing. There are people, men, and women, who have been there and done that, and they survived.

Chapter Ten

Benji's Story

A lot of times, it is mostly women who are marrying for a green card. In this case, it is a man who married for a green card. This young man married this older woman for a green card. She was the breadwinner; she was the woman who paid all the bills; she did all that. Now, most American women are known to be very masculine; they are very alpha female. So for the alpha female, they feel somewhat entitled to treat a man anyhow. If you want to diminish a man, take away his desire, take away the means by which he should provide for his family. It is a natural thing from the time God created the heavens and earth that men are hunters. The fact that this man cannot provide for his family means he cannot be the king; he cannot do what he is supposed to do as a man.

A man can assume the role of a housekeeper to make sure when she comes home, the house is clean, the dinner is cooked, her car is washed, etc. He makes up for where he cannot provide by doing everything around the house, everything. He does the domesticated part of it. He does the supermarket shopping; he is a gopher making sure everything is locked tight and everything. She married him; they were going to the embassy; she made sure all the papers were mailed in. That was one thing she did: she made sure whatever paperwork they asked for, she would provide it.

They met in Jamaica, where the food is very nice, and romance is hot and sizzling. She brought him to the US, and this man would vent to his friends how this woman treated him and how the woman talked to him. But he was still working on the marriage as a tangible marriage. He was working on it. Even though the green card was involved, he still loved her.

He was still catering to her; he loved her. So, the long and short of it is, his green card came in the mail eventually, and she took the green card and hid the green card in a jacket pocket in a clothes closet in the corner. He was the one who ironed everything because he was the one who did the laundry, so he ironed everything. He ironed her clothes, even those she wore to work. So he ironed everything and hung them in the closet.

One day, he was trying to make space in the closet to hang things. It was getting hot, so he was taking down some of the winter stuff to make room for the summer clothes. He took down this jacket and saw this paper sticking out of the pocket. He took the thing out of the pocket because it was already opened. He opened it, and the date was on it when it was mailed out, and his green card was in there. This man fell apart.

He called his best friend, who is the one who told the story. He told him about it, and he just stopped and paused right in his tracks. Instead of destroying everything in the house, instead of going crazy, all he did was write her a note, take the green card, take his passport and all the rest of his documents, and exit the building. This woman never saw or heard from him again. He filed for divorce and mailed her the paperwork.

I think he must have gone to a state and divorced her where divorces were uncontested. So the divorce was final; she knew nothing about it, and he moved on with his life.

What Benji experienced was abuse. This woman made him into an indentured servant, a personnel gopher; there was no reason for this. She saw no reason to make sure this man was moving about the country. What would cause her to do something like that?

People would say he was a "yard boy" in our Jamaican term. He was a poor thing; he was just doing the best he could, and that was what he got.

Now, you may see this man and ask him to send you money, and he looks at you and says he does not have it. You do not know what he did; you do not know what he went through to be where he is. You now know his story. This is Benji's story.

Chapter Eleven

When Desire Breeds Violence

On Thursday, April 9, 2015, there was a newspaper article titled "Man stabbed girlfriend at Metro-North train station in Irvington."

The article reads as follows:

> IRVINGTON, N.Y. (WABC) -- Police in Westchester County are investigating after a man allegedly stabbed his girlfriend... .
>
> According to police, the 52-year-old man was waiting at the train station

and attacked the 36-year old woman as she was on her way home.

The man stabbed the woman several times in the head, torso and leg, police said, then he slashed his own throat when confronted by responding officers.

The woman, from Yonkers, is in critical but stable condition. The man, from Mount Vernon, is in guarded condition.

The woman is alive thanks to the quick action of Irvington Fire Department Chief Chris DePaoli, who said he was driving by the incident and thought he saw a purse snatching.

"I yelled at the guy to get away from her and radioed in to police that there was an assault going on," he said.
Then he approached the two and realized it was a stabbing. DePaoli said

he went back and got a bat from his car, then threatened the suspect, telling him to leave the woman alone.

Within minutes the suspect was also confronted by an off-duty police officer and responding units.

The man began slashing his own neck until he was tasered.

Southbound Metro-North trains were not stopping at Irvington Wednesday evening while police investigated, but later resumed service.

As for what led up to the bloody confrontation, police say there was a domestic violence incident earlier this week. "There is a domestic incident report filed previously on Tuesday night after a Monday night event between the couple that was filed in a different jurisdiction and we believe he waited at the station and plotted his attack," said Insp. Joseph Martell of the MTA police department.

Charges against the suspect are pending.

Further investigations led to the following, "Mount Vernon Man Indicted on Attempted Murder Charges in Irvington Train Station Attack."

Village Fire Chief Chris DePaoli helped save the life of victim Deborah Henry, and he was honored at the state capitol for his efforts.

Sidney Brown, 51, of Mount Vernon was arraigned Thursday on a seven-count indictment charging him with attempted murder and related crimes in connection with his alleged April attack on his ex-girlfriend.

Westchester County District Attorney Janet DiFiore announced the indictments, outlining the brutal attack on victim Deborah Henry, who is the mother of Brown's children.

"This indictment outlines a frightening course of escalating violence by the defendant including constant harassment, intimidation and stalking," said DiFiore in a statement. "Ultimately the defendant waited for the victim at a commuter train station and attacked her in full view of numerous witnesses, if it wasn't for the intervention of several good Samaritans, the outcome would have been much worse."

As the investigation continued, even more revelation came to the fore about this particular case.

Mount Vernon Man, 51, Charged in Irvington Train Station Assault:

One count of Attempted Murder in the Second Degree, a class "B" Felony, one count of Assault in the First Degree, a class "B" Felony, one count of Assault in the Second Degree, a class "D" Felony, one count of Stalking in the First Degree a class "D" Felony, two counts of Criminal Possession of a Weapon in the Third Degree, class "E" Felonies, one count of Endangering the welfare of a Child, a class "A" Misdemeanor, one count of Aggravated Harassment, a class "A" Misdemeanor.

The incident, which was witnessed by numerous bystanders, occurred on April 8 in the parking lot of the Irvington train station. Brown is accused of attacking Henry, stabbing her repeatedly in the neck, torso, back, and thigh.

Irvington Fire Chief Chris DePaoli, who was driving by with his daughters, saw the alleged attack, jumped out of his truck, grabbed a baseball bat, and broke up the assault. Brown was arrested by police moments later.

DePaoli was honored at the state capitol by Sen. Andrea Stewart-Cousins for his efforts.

Brown and Henry had been domestic partners and have three children in common, according to DiFiore. Both were treated at local hospitals.

Two days after the attack, Brown was discharged from Westchester Medical Center and arraigned in Irvington Village Court.

He has a number of open arrest and bench warrants in Mount Vernon and Yonkers for domestic violence incidents involving both his current wife and Henry, DiFiore said. He remains remanded in jail.

Brown faces a maximum sentence of 25 years in state prison, and his case was adjourned to August 13.

Assistant District Attorney Wendy Parra, Chief of the Domestic Violence Bureau and Assistant District Attorney Karen Herbert of the Domestic Violence Bureau are prosecuting the case.

This was a domestic issue that escalated into a violent attack. At the core of this incident is the green card saga. It is apparent that this decision can lead to a violent confrontation. I have seen the desire for a green card manifest negatively at every possible level. We must begin our journey to healing and liberation, but above all, those of us who have experienced the brunt of this deal can see the truth in it and must be a voice of reason and dissuasion to our fellow brothers and sisters who think this is the way to a better life.

Chapter Twelve

Miss Vermont's Story

It was a long way from Jamaica, and she was promised a very lucrative job in the cold country of the United States of America, in the state of Vermont, where she was told that she would be working in the hotel industry as a housekeeper. Much to her surprise, when she got there, it was nothing like that.

She was basically a housekeeper at a motel, where there were truck drivers who passed through at night. Of course, prostitutes frequented the truck stop with the truck drivers, where they would solicit the truck drivers with the intention of giving them sex for money. It was quite a shock to her that these things went on right under the nose of passengers who were sleeping in their cars at a rest stop. It was a shock to her as well that this would go on night in and night out, all in the name of getting a green card. Also, they would give her a room, at the same place on the hotel premises, much to her surprise. It was a roof over her head.

In her mind, she was not one of those persons who had to sleep with roommates or sleep on someone's floor or in a shelter or something like that. It was not what she was promised, but because she had so much on the line, and so much things in Jamaica, so many people waiting for her, not knowing what she was going through, she thought it was the best thing for them that they did not know what she was going through. So she kept them in the dark and just put her head down and did what she had to do like a lot of people who come to America having no idea what they are coming to, and they are usually promised so much. She just did what she had to do.

The job lasted for almost a year and a half. I am still not sure what she did because she did not want to talk about it much, but I got enough from her to share with you. Prepare yourself for what is going to come if you decide to leave Jamaica or any country you live in to come to this country with the intention that it is easy. The United States is no bed of roses for immigrants.

After the project was over, she left that job and took another job. It was pretty much the same thing, except it was a bigger hotel. It was nicer. It was not a motel. She got away from the truck stop, and now she was working in a hotel. The work was hard, but she was able to have better food. I believe that if you at least have good food, your body will be properly nourished, and you can probably work better. So she kept that job.

During the time she was at this job working, a gentleman saw her. She was from Jamaica, so yes, she was a melanin sister. She met this gentleman, and he wooed her; he was a businessman. He visited the hotel all the time to stay. If she was not at work, he would ask for her. He was in town often because that was where he did business, and he would sleep at the same hotel. He kept asking for her, and she thought he was joking. They would just talk from time to time, if she ran into him or if he saw her. It came time for her to leave, and she went to tell him goodbye.

"You're leaving?"

"Yes, I'm leaving in two days."

"No, you're not."

"Yes, I am."

"What can I do for you not to leave?"

"Nothing. My time is up. The contract that I signed to be here is up in two days, and I have to go back home."

He said, "You know what can be done?"

"If I don't go back home, I have to go to another branch hotel and work."

"You are not leaving here, and you are not going home."

He took her to the Notary Public at the courthouse, and they got married. Today, they have two beautiful boys and a dog, a white picket fence, and a house on the lake. They are doing just wonderful. So, yes, this one indeed did work. He got her papers, gave her documents, and she never had to go back to Jamaica. She never had to do those contract works anymore. So that worked out very well for her.

So that is the story for this girl. We are going to call her Miss Vermont.

Chapter Thirteen

Mrs. Promiscuous

A businessman met this woman, and they were good friends for years. He thought that she would be 100% upfront with him about any and everything. They have been friends that long. Yes, friends can be lovers, and lovers can be best friends. He told her he would help her get her papers.

The fact that all her family was in Jamaica, she needed help, and he had the wherewithal to help. He had businesses. Financially, he was stable. He was able to help her, not just financially, but he was able to give her documents.

It was not all about a green card for her; she secretly had a crush on him. They decided to take it to the next level. She would visit his business place and bring him dinner. She would do his laundry if needs be, but he would not tell her that he liked her, nor would she tell him that she liked him. She would go to his business place, help out with everything. She would stay there with him late at night until the establishment closed, and there were no strings attached; they were just friends.

They would hang out more often than not, and there were times she would not go home. Whenever he left work at nights, he would drop her off. She would come there early in the morning, and she would leave late at night. That spoke volumes to his ego. He knew she liked him.

They went to the movies, then went for dinner. At dinner, she professed her love for him at the table, and that was when he started to pursue her for a relationship. It so happened that they indeed started a relationship. She would spend even more time at his business place.

He ultimately fell in love with her, and they got married at the justice of the peace. They were inseparable. They were like two peas in a pod. At one point, she was a churchgoer, and he started going to church with her. He too was a churchgoer. They continued going to church together.

At some point, the marriage hit a rough patch. They worked through it. It escalated again to some more issues. They would not tell me who was messing up, but they both owned up to the fact that they were struggling in the marriage. Of course, all marriages go through ups and downs, but it is how you handle it. They were going through their little ups and downs, and no one would take the blame.

I guess one would try to blame the other, so it became the blame game, but they still tried to work through it.

At this point, she wanted a baby. He did not want any more children. I guess that was what started eating away at the marriage. There was this time where she felt as though she missed her menstrual cycle, and he decided to take her to the doctor. They went to the doctor together. They ran some tests on her; they ran some tests on him. When they were going to get the test results, they had to ask permission for the other person to be in the room. In this case, even though that was her husband, she still could hear her test results without him. They brought her into the room, and they sat her down. They explained to her about her labs. However, they told her that one of the labs came back abnormal.

I am pretty sure she thought it was the pregnancy, as if the pregnancy test were a part, but they told her no. They asked her if she wanted them to call her husband. She told them no. That was when they told her that she was HIV positive.

What are we willing to do for a green card? She lost it. She cried. She sobbed. The doctor asked her if she could tell him herself. She said, no, she wanted them to tell him.

They went back outside, and they got him and pulled him back into a room. They told him that she was HIV positive and that they had to do some labs on him. They ran the test on him, and it came back negative. He decided that he was going to stick it out with his wife; he was going to stay with her. They were going to work through it.

They started doing what prevention they needed to take. What were the protocols? How is this going to go going forward? What did they need to do? They started taking precautions. She started taking her medicine, until the disease could not be detected in her body anymore. Everything started going well. Eventually, she started cheating. She just went back to her old pattern, maybe because there was anger. She did not know where she got the disease because her husband was negative. So, quite naturally, she got it from someone else.

She became promiscuous. She was not promiscuous in the States, but when she went to Jamaica, she was just carrying on. Her husband found out that she was sleeping with multiple persons. He contacted these persons and asked about it. Did they know she was HIV positive? These guys did not know; these guys did not have a clue.

This went on until he tracked all these men down who had slept with her without protection. He eventually divorced her and moved on with his life. He remarried and is living happily ever after. He now has a beautiful wife. They are doing amazing.

He did the right thing because he did not know if she was going to continue to be promiscuous and re-infect herself, and you can indeed get re-infected.

So the price of giving a green card, the price of marrying somebody for one can be costly to your life. It can be costly, and you can get used. It is just a bad thing. It is really, really a bad thing.

Chapter Fourteen

Green Card Hustle

The issue of a green card is not exclusive to the heathen; it extends even within the four walls of the church. Let us take it a little bit to the church. I really want to understand what some older women are thinking when they marry younger men in the church. I think it is just simply ludicrous.

It is very unfair and selfish in a sense that nine out of ten times they marry these younger men who do not have any children. Some of these women have already tied their tubes; they have had different kinds of tubal ligation; some of them have had a complete hysterectomy and know full well that they will never conceive; it is impossible for them to have any children. Yet they want to marry these young boys. Then after they do these marriages, they want God to do a miracle. He is not going to do a miracle, sweetheart, when your tubes are tied and burned. He is not going to do a miracle when you do not have a uterus; there is no miracle for Him to do there.

I am going to put some of the blame too on some of these young boys who meet these older women. They are just so persistent because you will tell them no a million times, and they do not quit. Oh, I will just live with it. Oh, I will adopt. We do not need to have any children until three years in the relationship. That is all they talk about. They want to have children.

Well, when we started talking, I did not want any kids. You said you were fine with it. You said we could adopt. Then three years later, you are telling me about children. Sometimes that is the case. Sometimes some of these older women tell these men that they can in fact have children. That is unfair.

Young men, you guys can keep it together and hold on until you meet the wife that God has for you; the one with whom you can procreate with. Yes, indeed, you are going to want your own biological children in the future. What you want today, you will not want it next week. I can assure you of that.

It makes a lot of sense for you to just simply wait and be of good courage. God is going to send you a wife.

The divorce rate in the church is extremely high. Most of the time, it is worse in the church because of this same very thing. These younger men see older women come to Jamaica, and their skin is on fire. They just want to get married because they are in love.

They are in love with the smell of the irish spring. They are in love with the smell of fresh clothes and the fabric softener. That is what they are so in love with. They are in love with this idea of marrying a powerful woman in church. So by the time they get over all that and come to the reality that they were not as in love as they thought, they are already in a committed marriage. Then you are unhappy, and she is unhappy. Everybody in the world knows about it.

The green card costs a whole lot of women their lives. It costs a whole lot of men their lives, and for what? A lot of people live in misery right now because of the green card. Others will just now walk away because of the green card. The divorce rate could be so much less, especially in the church, because a lot of green card marriage is going on in there. These young boys want to marry these older women. By the time they get to America, they realize that they cannot stay with someone who cannot give them children. That is one of their ways to escape. They want to have children. When they pull that "I want to have kids" card, they know we are not going to fight with them, and that is their way to escape. That is the way to leave.

I want to reiterate this; you make sure that you are marrying for the right reason because too many people who commit suicide after people use them for green card have lost everything. People kill people who have taken a green card from them, and they feel used and abused. People lose their lives for this. It is not worth it. It is certainly not worth it.

These are all stories, but they serve as a warning as well.

Chapter Fifteen

Children Suffer Too

Those who pursue a green card are often forgotten, hurt, and damaged, for they are the ones who feel it most of all, and the ones who are silent. No one acts on their behalf or takes the time out to help.

It only requires one look in their eyes to find out the long-term psychological damage that happened to these people as society continues to perpetuate the same hurt unto them year after year, month after month, decade after decade because they want to go after the American dream. The really damaged people are the children of potential immigrants in the grand scheme of things. They are the ones who end up on the affected end of the stick where one person's going after the American dream with this hope and happy dreams and the glee to go into a country where they think opportunity is. A lot of the times, they do not know that everything is not for free and life is not easy. There is no happy-go-lucky and ice cream with the cherry on the top; a club here and a club there. That is not what it is.

The affected children can understand and process the fact that they are going to grow up without a mother, or they are going to grow up without a father, because their mother or father sometimes hold on to false dreams and hopes that the children are going to join their parents in America in a year or so, depending on how old they are. They feel like they are also going to partake in the American dream and join mom or dad. Maybe it is an aunt, or whoever is raising them; the thought is, migrating illegally is only temporary; they are going to be back soon. They will not be gone for a long time.

Years go by, and the memories sometimes fade. Some children still wait for years, and after a while, they are being abused or lack so much. Nine out of ten times items are sent to Jamaica for these children, and they never get it. If you send twelve pencils, they are lucky if they get three. They are the ones who truly suffer. They are the ones who grow up resenting their parents because what they did makes no sense them.

Sometimes some of these parents come to America or go to a foreign country, and it did not pan out the way they thought it was going to. No one explained to the children, and these parents are stuck in these foreign countries and are never able to go back home. They feel so guilty. The guilt is so much that they start believing that the children will not remember them, and they are just going to forget everything about them, so it is best not to just go back in their lives and hurt them again. They sometimes choose to continue living their lives; turn a new page and never go back.

Parents do not know how to explain their dilemma to their kids. Some parents try to buy and send things, believing that they can buy the child. They think if they send enough things, it will fill the void, and the child will forgive. They think if they can get in a position to sponsor this child to come to America or come to this foreign country, then they will forgive.

Sometimes the filing for the child will come through, and they will bring the child to America or to the foreign country where they are. When the child gets there, there is another hurdle to cross because this child does not remember them. The child resents them, hates them, and then you have a very tumultuous relationship between parents and child because you left for so long and there is so much that happened, that this child had gone through so many hurdles in their life at a time when they needed you the most. It is here that therapy needs to begin, so the child can understand that the mother did not leave because she wanted to; she left to make a better life for them.

The parent/child needs to understand that they might not forgive you at the same time, but give them something to work with. Bridge the gap in here. Do not go back to your yelling and screaming at the child. Everybody is yelling because they do not see you as a mother anymore. Just let time heal, because, in retrospect, you really were not there.

The immigrant children who are left behind are damaged, and we cannot overlook how damaged they are with some gift from Santa when Christmas comes. We cannot forgive how damaged they are if we take them outside and make some snowman and hit them with the snow if they come in the wintertime. We cannot put a band-aid on a third-degree cut. These children of immigrant parents are left behind in a foreign country from where the parents leave them. Sometimes they suffer and they suffer a great deal in the same way that the parent who leaves with the intention to come right back also suffers. It was not what they thought it would be. They suffer as well.

It does not make it better for the parent or for the child to understand, but it starts the healing process, and they bridge the gap.

The parents who leave their children behind will suffer double for leaving their children behind because of what they face when they are here on farm work, and their visa expires.

Chapter Sixteen

A Word To Those Thinking About Running Off

We are planted where God wants us to be, and the goal for us is to come into our identity and bloom where we are planted. If God wanted us in another country, we would have been born and bred there. If our divine purpose requires us to relocate, then a legal opportunity will present ourselves to make this happen.

We often open the windows to a perpetual nightmare by taking matters into our own hands and making what we desire happen for ourselves without thought of timing and legality.

The idea that the grass is greener on the other side is a misguided myth that has plunged many headlong into living nightmares that they do not wake up from. I would not want that for you, and I believe I speak for everyone whose story you have read so far.

Here are some key points from the CIS website to consider:

- Marriage to an American citizen remains the most common path to U.S. residency and/or citizenship for foreign nationals, with more than 2.3 million foreign nationals gaining lawful permanent resident (LPR) status in this manner between 1998 and 2007.

- More than 25 percent of all green cards issued in 2007 were to the spouses of American citizens. In 2006 and 2007 there were nearly twice as many green cards issued to the spouses of American citizens than were issued for all employment-based immigration categories combined. The number of foreign nationals obtaining green cards based on marriage to an American has more than doubled since 1985, and has quintupled since 1970.

- Despite these statistics, marriage fraud for the purpose of immigration gets very little notice or debate in the public arena and the State Department and Department of Homeland Security have nowhere near the resources needed to combat the problem. Attention to fraud is not just for the integrity of the legal immigration system, but also for security reasons.

If small-time con artists and Third-World gold-diggers can obtain green cards with so little resistance, then surely terrorists can do (and have done) the same.

- An overwhelming percentage of all petitions to bring foreign spouses or fiancés to the United States illegally (or to help them adjust visa status if they are already in the United States on non-immigrant visas) are approved—even in cases where the couple may only have met over the Internet, and may not even share a common language.

- Marriage to an American is the clearest pathway to citizenship for an illegal alien. A substantial number of illegal aliens ordered removed (many of whom have criminal records) later resurface as marriage-based green card applicants. Waivers granted to those marrying U.S. citizens can eliminate ineligibilities for green cards, including the 3/10-year bar on entry for those with long periods of illegal presence.

- The decision-making authority for green card applications lies with USCIS officials who rely almost exclusively on documents, records, and photographs, with little opportunity for interviews or investigations. Consular officers reviewing cases overseas do live interviews and can initiate local investigations, but may only approve petitions, not deny them.[1]

This source continues to say:

Since 1998, more than 2.3 million foreign nationals have obtained green cards

---

[1]https://cis.org/Report/Inside-Green-Card-Marriage-Phenomenon

through marriage to American citizens. (See Tables 1 and 2.) Nearly a million more have obtained green cards through marriage to LPRs.

The question is, is it worth it?

Too many people have fallen into this trap, and because of pride and embarrassment, they never tell their stories. Immigrants are treated like outsiders in another country, no matter how welcoming they seem initially. They will smile with you, but make sure you have a low job that no citizens want to do. They will slave you out, use you, abuse you, and reject you if you no longer serve a purpose.

Even those who have gotten a green card by this means many times end up having to start over from scratch. They suffer, those they leave behind in their home country suffer, and they live out their nightmares in secret.

If you want to migrate, let your petition and request be made known to God, and allow Him to provide the means and opportunity to do it the right way.

You are in control of your own life and destiny. If you choose to go after a green card by providing the opportunity yourself, you surrender control of your life, and you become a slave to the one who can provide what you so desire. Do not get caught in that trap.

Chapter Seventeen

A Word To Those Who Have Already Run Off

Options to get your legal status are very limited. One train of thought is to find a good lawyer who can advise you. If you see marriage as the only alternative, try to develop an authentic love relationship, and not just get married for papers. It can seem heavenly initially, but can quickly escalate into a hell, so spend the time to get to know the person.

According to CitizenPath.com, there are four paths to take for undocumented immigrants. This is what they had to say:

For undocumented immigrants in the United States, life can be difficult. The stakes are high. Getting caught means a likely removal (deportation) from the United States. But it also may break apart a family, disrupt the family's finances, and result in stiffer immigration penalties. Currently, there is no extensive amnesty program like President Reagan introduced in 1986, but there are a variety of smaller programs that offer paths to legal status for certain undocumented immigrants.

For undocumented immigrants, the clear goal is a path to a long-term legal status. These paths to legal status lead to permanent residence (green card) and U.S. citizenship. Certain immigrants with no legal status may have some paths available. This article covers those options and who could qualify for them.

In this article, the term "undocumented" immigrant is used to describe an immigrant without any legal immigration status. No status may be the result of entering the United States without inspection or entering via a legal non-immigrant visa (e.g. tourist visa, student visa) that has since expired. The term "entered without inspection" or EWI is used to specifically describe someone that has come across the border and never interacted with a U.S. border agent.

Although there are approximately 650,000 childhood arrivals protected by the DACA program, this is not a lawful immigration status. It is a temporary solution and provides extremely limited opportunities for the beneficiaries. DACA recipients need paths to legal status like any other undocumented individual. Although not everyone will qualify for these paths, they are worth learning about:

1. *Green Card through Marriage to a U.S. Citizen or LPR*

2. *DREAMers Green Card through Employment with LIFE Act Protection.*

3. *Asylum Status*

4. *U Visa for Victims of Crime[2]*

Most undocumented immigrants seek option 1, which led to many of the horror stories you have read in this book.

The damage has already been done: you have already run off, so your options are

---

[2]https://citizenpath.com/paths-to-legal-status-undocumented/

limited. Either find one of these four ways to get your documents, or resolve to go back to your home country with no possibility of ever entering the United States again. It is a very uncomfortable dilemma to find oneself in, and it is my prayer that this is not where you are caught at the reading of this book. If it is, know there are options, but beware.

Chapter Eighteen

Maintaining the Integrity of Your Soul

It is important to only engage in the legal way of doing things because all other alternatives may give us a false sense of safety, but come to bite us one day well into the future.

It is clear that not only those who make the decision to leave their country illegally suffer but those who get left behind, particularly the children. The relationship is often severed beyond repair, and while there may be opportunities of sourcing a viable income, the price paid far outweighs the benefits derived, so one must think carefully before making such a decision.

While it is expected that those who have a secular background have no need to maintain the integrity of their souls because they are not guided by the same moral compass as those who are believers in Christ, it is disheartening to learn that believers are also making the same decisions, while holding to the fact that their integrity is intact. It is not. Taking an illegal route to create opportunities for yourself is a serious compromise to your integrity, and you don't want that to be on your record in heaven.

God has called us to live above the systems and cultures of this world, because our citizenship is in another world. Integrity is a big deal to God, though many ignore this because they act contrary to God's nature, and don't experience an immediate consequence. Doing the right thing will always pay off in the end. Doing the wrong thing can seem innocent at first, but will show up again in the future because every act is a seed planted to be harvested in a future time.

Maintaining the integrity of your soul secures a good and prosperous future for you and your family.

Epilogue

I will end on this note: you are a valuable commodity, but bad decisions can cause you to see yourself as less-than. Some bad decisions can be reversed, though the consequences remain; while some bad decisions are irreversible, and the repercussions extend well beyond future years.

You can avoid certain pitfalls and traps by carefully considering the pros and cons of such a serious decision as to run off in a foreign country. Your illegal status gives you limited access to the freedom you so desire, and you will spend your time hiding and counting the cost for every decision you make going forward because of what is at risk. Certainly, the mental and psychological strain of living such a life is not worth the decision to go after it.

The greatest power we have is our capacity to choose. Sometimes we surrender that power by making one bad decision. We must carefully consider our options before making a life-altering decision as those in the stories you have read. Sometimes we choose to see the outcome we want to see in order to blind ourselves from the obvious truth so we can make certain decisions. This is never a good idea.

We create our lives by the choices we make, and the reality of life is this: Whatever bed we spread, we are the ones who will have to lie in it.

References

https://patch.com/new-york/rivertowns/mount-vernon-man-indicted-attempted-murder-charges-irvington-train-station-attack

https://abc7ny.com/metro-north-stabbing-investigation/644093/

Other Books by the Author

Mom, Are You Scared?
It is never easy to lose someone you love dearly due to a terminal illness. Losing a loved one as a result of AML Leukemia, has left many, including Donette Wright, feeling as though they would never be able to laugh or be happy again. It poses the question that many may ask, "Will my life ever be the same?"

Donette's mother was a matriarch, who was the glue that kept her family together. When she passed away Donette shares how she went into a state of isolation. Her home became her prison. It is always painful to let your loved ones go, but this book will help you know that you will be able to overcome the pain of losing someone that you loved dearly. Let's embrace the good memories we have and move beyond the dark painful battle they had to endure. You will laugh again!

Available on Amazon.com